Secrets to Attaining College Success

2nd ed

Neil O'Donnell

Secrets to Attaining College Success, 2nd ed © All rights reserved by Neil O'Donnell

No part of this book may be reproduced or transmitted in any form or by any means, graphic, electronic, or mechanical, including photocopying, recording, taping, or by any informational storage retrieval system without prior permission in writing from the publisher.

W & B Publishers

For information:
W & B Publishers
Post Office Box 193
Colfax, NC 27235
www.a-argusbooks.com

ISBN:978-0-6923082-5-7
ISBN: 0-6923082-5-3

Book Cover designed by Dubya

Printed in the United States of America

Neil O'Donnell

Neil O'Donnell is an Anthropologist with specializations in Medical Anthropology, Prehistoric Archaeology and Socio-Cultural Anthropology. A certified Master Tutor Trainer, with additional certifications in Career Coaching and Stress Management, Neil has over twenty years of experience in developing and providing academic, career and personal support to college students and alumni.

O'Donnell is also an award winning author whose publications include novels, nonfiction books, short stories, and peer-reviewed articles for journals and volumes which include North American Archaeologist, The Association for the Tutoring Profession, The Encyclopedia of Anthropology, The Encyclopedia of Time, and 21st Century Anthropology. Through the writing of his memoir, Bellwood, OCD and Me and presentations funded by the Center for Development of Human Services (CDHS), Neil focuses much of his free time educating the community about Obsessive-compulsive Disorder.

O'Donnell is a member of multiple professional organizations including the American College Counseling Association, the American Counseling Association, the Association for the Tutoring Profession, the Register of Professional Archaeologists, the New York State Archaeological Association, and the Northeastern Anthropological Association.

Table of Contents

Chapter 1…Welcome to College-------------------- 1

Chapter 2…Getting Ready to Succeed--------------- 7

Chapter 3…Note-taking Strategies----------------- 34

Chapter 4…Class Participation Do's and Don'ts -- 53

Chapter 5…Reading Strategies That Work---------- 62

Chapter 6…Writing an "A" Research Paper--------- 80

Chapter 7…Test Preparations & Success------------ 96

Chapter 8…Organizing Effective Study Group----- 108

Chapter 9…Utilize Available Support Services----- 117

Chapter 10..Money Management Basics------------- 124

Chapter 11..Final Advice for Attaining Success---- 138

Acknowledgements

This edition is dedicated to my parents, Edward and Maureen O'Donnell, both of whom sacrificed so much so that my siblings and I could have a good life. We love and miss you Mom and Dad, every day.

Chapter 1

Welcome to College

You got into college, so now what? Well first of all, congratulations! Not just for getting into an institution of higher education, but also because you recognized the importance of education beyond high school. As for which type of higher education you should pursue, it all depends on the career path you seek. Those pursuing a career path in auto mechanics, carpentry, culinary arts, masonry, or plumbing can often gain the required skill sets and experience through trade schools, community colleges and/or apprenticeship programs. For careers requiring graduate degrees (Master's, Ph.D., MD, etc.), a Bachelor's degree is required necessitating coursework at a four-year institution or university (though getting an Associate's at a community college could provide a good, cost-effective start for many). Bottom-line, the importance for all students is the focus on gaining a higher-level of education, and for the record, a student's education doesn't end after attaining a degree. Most fields require ongoing or "continuing" education in the form of workshops and/or refresher courses.

Now, whether a student is attending a community college, a four-year college or a university, the advice contained herein should provide a great foundation for attaining academic and personal success. It's funny, students hear about the importance of a college education, but how often do teachers, parents and mentors push the idea of learning college-level study skills? Sure, a lot of colleges discuss these things in freshmen orientation, but often that is the only instruction in study and success skills students receive. That is the reason behind this book. I wanted all students to have a straightforward guide to skill sets that would make it easier to attain A's in college courses right from the get-go. Where do the strategies come from? The suggested strategies are tried and true techniques I used and have been sharing with college students for over twenty years. As a professional tutor, I spent a tremendous amount of time teaching students these techniques, and those students choosing to implement these strategies often found great academic and personal success as a result. Likewise, as a Master Tutor Trainer, I have taught other tutors these techniques so they could share them with their students. Again, students in turn were often successful when following through and utilizing the strategies laid out in the following chapters.

So why is it so crucial to use these techniques? Does it truly matter if a student has an A average verses a C average? That may seem like a silly question, but it's one that students and parents ask a lot. In response, let me say just a couple things. First, the study strategies presented here generally help students better learn and RETAIN information from textbooks and class discussions/lectures (notes). Think about it. If a student spends thousands of dollars on an education, attains a C average, gets a degree, but he or she retains relatively little knowledge, is that a good investment? Believe it or not, a lot of what is covered in classes will be of use in the real world. Those who don't remember skills won't likely be employed long. Consequently, it definitely makes sense to retain as much information as possible, which is Argument 1 for learning good study skills. Next, consider the goal of obtaining a degree.

Many jobs today require applicants to have a college degree, often a minimum of a Bachelor's. Do you think a college is just going to hand out a degree? No, students need to pass their classes, and that means the students need to learn and retain class material. This provides the second argument in support of learning study skills such as those presented in this text.

Wait, are you still questioning the importance of learning study skills? Okay, here's a final argument.

To get into graduate school, college graduates often need to have a minimum GPA of a 3.0. Furthermore, some employers do ask for college transcripts and look at grades when considering whether or not to hire someone. Grades do matter in a lot of instances. How does a student get good grades? Again, good study habits and strategies are what make a difference as no one to my knowledge has perfected a way to learn and retain information simply by sitting in a classroom. Bottom-line, to increase the likelihood of graduating, gaining a job or entrance into graduate school, and/or leaving college with a wealth of practical skill sets, a student must truly learn and retain information. In other words, learn and implement some or all of the following techniques to increase the likelihood of graduating and having a successful career.

Chapter 2

Getting Ready to Succeed

I'm not going to tell you that college is easy, because it's not. That said, college and its associated coursework are very manageable as long as a student is willing to invest time into her or his studies. No, I'm not advocating that a student spend every hour of every day studying class notes or reading textbooks in order to achieve success. I'm simply advising students to spend a sufficient amount of time each week devoted to their studies in and out of the classroom. What's a sufficient amount of time to spend studying? We'll get in to that shortly. First, I wanted to put things into perspective. How much are you spending on your education? Between tuition, supplies, a dorm room and pens, I'm betting it's a small fortune. If you don't invest time into college along with the money, it's going to be difficult to ultimately pass classes and get a degree. If you don't have a degree, how are you going to get a job and pay off any loans? You see the dilemma college students face?

With that said, let's get you prepared to succeed. What's first? You need to gather a few tools, and you need to start stockpiling materials as soon as you are registered for classes. As for essentials, while completing a Bachelor's and Master's and after tutoring/advising countless students since 1992, I've found the following tools crucial for success:

- **A notebook for each class**. I preferred a 3-inch binder with loose-leaf paper and dividers separating a section for each class, but a five-subject notebook or individual wire-bound notebooks work fine. I strongly recommend college-ruled paper in either case. That said, I know several friends and students who prefer wide-ruled; get whichever works best for you.

- **A small, wire-bound notebook for writing down miscellaneous notes and/or assignments. <u>The sooner you get in the habit of carrying this around, the better.</u>** As a writer, I often carry around a notebook for writing down plot ideas and character traits/names. As a student, such a notebook is useful for writing down questions you want to ask a professor or ideas a student comes up with for a paper's thesis.

- **A small, "collegiate" dictionary.** I still have the dictionary Buffalo State's EOP Program gave me in 1989, which remains one of the greatest/most valuable tools I ever received. As for non-collegiate dictionaries, students will generally find such resources limited so it is worth the extra few dollars for the collegiate dictionary.

- **A daily planner.** Preferably one that has space to write down specifics about class assignments. The kicker here is that a student finds a planner and USES the planner.

- **Several pens and pencils.** Always carry spares and try to have a mechanical pencil on hand, because you usually can't sharpen pencils during the middle of class.

- **A folder for each class in which to store class syllabi, handouts, and returned assignments, quizzes or examinations.** Folders are an easy way to get and stay organized especially during preparation for final exams.

- **A scientific calculator.** Math and science majors should consult with department advisors to determine an appropriate calculator. Those majors requiring calculus or other advanced math courses might want to consider a graphic calculator.

- **A ruler with centimeters and inches.** I prefer metrics, but most of my professors required measurements in inches.

- **A stapler that uses standard-sized staples. Small/compact staplers are fine as long as they use "standard" staples.** Staples less than standard size struggle to pierce through anything that's more than five pages. Additionally, finding replacement staples for out-sized staples is difficult.

- **A good supply of post-it notes.** For leaving notes on refrigerators, in notebooks or in textbooks, nothing beats a post-it note as far as I'm concerned as they allow for marking a page without writing in a text and easily returning to an important page in a book.

- **A pack of standard paperclips.** A box containing 250-500 paperclips should be fine and carry through your entire undergraduate career.

- **A pencil sharpener.** A small, manual one that collects shavings is perfect for bringing to class.

- **A large eraser**. I've always found that the little nub of an eraser on pencils never lasts long. A kneaded eraser or a standard 1" by .5" eraser should get you through a semester if not an academic year.

- **A hole-puncher.** Preferably one that punches three holes at once. As an FYI, it's worth spending a few dollars more to get a good hole-puncher as the cheap ones break easily and/or can only punch a few pages at a time.

- **A role of scotch tape.** Though I rarely used it, scotch tape was handy for repairing folders and sticking notes/reminders to doors or walls without leaving permanent marks. And, just in case you need to rebind a book or tape together your book bag in an emergency, keep a roll of duct tape on hand as well.

- **A flash/thumb drive specifically for storing papers and other class-related assignments.** Keep a separate flash drive for computer science or digital media classes. Back up files daily (I lost five chapters of my Master's Thesis by ignoring this rule). Also, many freshmen receive a free flash drive during summer orientation. While it's cool to get a flash drive for free and with the college's logo on it, these flash drives rarely last a long time. I recommend students purchase a name brand flash drive (Kingston and Lexar are my personal favorites).

- **A roll of quarters.** No, this is not something a student needs to carry 24/7. Keep this tucked away for an emergency to pay for bus fare, a few stamps, photocopies, and vending machine snacks.

- **A backpack or other type of bag to carry supplies in.** Select a bag that will withstand inclement weather such as rain and snow (I guess I should mention I live in Buffalo). Also try to find something with separate compartments as storing pens in the same space as papers could lead to stray pen marks all over a research paper.

- **A large, plastic tote to store all class notes, exams, papers, etc.** This will serve as a storage unit that is resistant to moisture from surprise floods or infestation from rodents or bugs. At the end of every semester, place notebooks, syllabi and tests in the tote. Save everything until after you graduate in case you have to dispute a grade. Saving course syllabi is especially important in the event a graduate school or employer asks for a description of a course you completed.

[Notice I didn't list a highlighter! I'll explain why later.]

Aside from the tote, you should keep the above supplies on hand at all times. If you live on campus, you can store books and any unneeded equipment in your room; commuters can store things in their car trunk or in a campus locker in the commuter lounge if available. The reason for keeping these supplies close? Paying for or locating a stapler, a hole-puncher, pens or other necessities can be costly and/or time consuming on campus.

Stress-Relief Tools for College Success

As a certified Stress Management Coach, I find that students and college personnel fail to equip themselves for the stress and anxiety that comes with college life. For students who don't prepare to handle college stress, academic success is an even greater challenge. Consequently, I added an additional list of supplies here to prepare students for those days when bad grades surface, workload frustration mounts or loneliness strikes, and this list includes:

- **A quiet space to study.** Whether it's a corner of the campus library, your dorm room or the basement of your family home, all students need a quiet space in which to study. If it's your dorm room, set aside "quiet time" with any roommates to assure there will be no distractions and put that in a roommate contract. This quiet time/space will help you focus on your studies. While I know a lot of students think music helps them study, this is generally untrue; these distractions will make it hard for you to concentrate on the work at hand. Have silence when you are studying notes, reading textbook chapters, and writing papers. Furthermore, establish quiet hours for sleeping so you can get uninterrupted sleep, a hot commodity for those seeking to reduce stress. By the way, if your dorm is your quiet space, keep it clean. Otherwise, you will struggle to find comfort in the room.

- **A journal for recording events and accomplishments.** It wasn't until I actually started journaling that I found out how much writing reduced stress. It was my second year as an undergraduate when I started and found a journal as a way to relieve stress and provide me with focus. I didn't write things down every day, but rather recorded accomplishments and things I learned from my missteps throughout each semester. There is no right way or wrong way to use a journal. Just record what you think is important; you will find your way and see how relaxing journaling can be.

- **A plant.** Dorm rooms are especially dull environments in which comfort is hard to come by. Adding a plant can bring a sense of comfort especially if the plant is an offshoot from a family plant like a flowering cactus or spider plant. A plant will help a dorm room feel a little like home. FYI – Jade and spider plants are very durable plants suited for those like me who can't handle high maintenance plants.

- **A small photo album.** Keeping an album of photos at hand is a great stress-relief tool. When I am having a tough day, I find a great deal of comfort and relieve a tremendous amount of stress by looking through photos of family, friends, happy events like weddings, or even just pictures of my family home.

- **A Zen garden.** Admittedly, I was skeptical of sand and rock gardens as well as desktop fountains. Frankly, I thought they were hokey when I was an undergrad. Now, as a professional, I find it quite relaxing to take a few minutes here and there to draw patterns in my desktop Zen garden with the little rakes included with the garden kit.

- **Dvds of your favorite movies.** Tough days come to every college student, and sometimes it's necessary to step away from the chaos of studies. Movies provide a great release at such difficult times so make certain you have a couple of your favorite movies on hand just in case.

- **A stress ball.** It's amazing how much relief one can get from squeezing the daylights out of a stress ball. Don't believe me? Buy one and squeeze the hell out of it when you're stressed. They're an inexpensive tool that will provide most with great relief.

Time Management

Now, equipment in hand, it is time to move on to the next step towards success at college; learning to manage your time. Earlier I recommended that students obtain a daily planner, which is a handy device for recording assignment due dates or exam dates/locations. If you followed my advice, it's time to take things a step further; you need to actually *use* the daily planner. I am always amazed at the number of students that purchase a daily planner, but never actually use it. I was guilty of this my first academic year of college. At my orientation, I received a nice daily planner with room for recording everything from my class times to final exam details. Months after I graduated, I found that planner at the bottom of a plastic tote I used to store papers in; I'd never used it. My mistake, a mistake I urge you not to make. Why? Planners obviously are great places to record information about class times, due dates and other scheduling details. Yet, there is a larger picture that students and professionals in all fields often overlook. Daily planners, when used routinely, help us to become more efficient with our time. Time is a preciously limited commodity we have. Unfortunately, we have a lot of responsibilities, and remembering and allowing time for every task and assignment is difficult to do. Hence, all students need to master Time Management as quickly as possible. To that end, I recommend the following tips, which helped me learn to manage my time and excel at college.

- **Obtain a daily planner.** You can purchase one at a bookstore or even print out one from the internet. Important thing here is to then use the planner and carry it with you at all times.

- **Record your name and an email address where you can be reached if someone finds/recovers it.** DO NOT write important personal information in the planner such as your social security number or a credit card number, because not everyone is trustworthy. If you misplace your planner or it's stolen, someone would have access to any information you put in there.

- **Record times you have classes.** Include info on the building and room the class is in. It's best to do this as soon as you register for courses. Why? You'd be amazed at how many students forget about class times and room numbers, especially during the first week of each semester.

- **After you receive your course syllabi, record important dates in your planner such as assignment due dates, days on which exams occur, etc.** There's nothing worse than not having access to a syllabus over a vacation and you can't remember when an assignment is due. If such information is in your planner, it's easy to look up that vital information.

- **Record information about days when college is closed for holidays.** It's important information to know **AND,** personally, I always got excited seeing "no classes" in my planner. It's also important to write down general college deadlines such as the last day to Withdraw from a class or the last day to add/drop classes.

Yes, I understand you were expecting more here. However, after decades of working with students, I've learned it's necessary to start small when it comes to time management, because MOST students have never paid much attention to it. Listing all the things that ultimately should be placed in a planner would be like throwing a non-swimmer into the deep end of the pool for the first lesson. Follow the above guidelines and give it a chance. It takes most people quite a while to get the hang of time management, so don't get frustrated if you forget to write down the due date for an assignment or if you forget to look over what you wrote and end up forgetting about a research paper. It happens even to the most dedicated professionals. Just keep at it, and eventually you will find your comfort zone. Maybe you will use your planner for only listing exams or for research papers. The important thing is to get into a HABIT of managing your time.

Now, as you get more adept at managing your time, here are additional things to set time aside for in your planner, which will be useful beyond your college years.

- **Write notes down in Saturday and Sunday spaces reminding you of what is due during the next week.** Include reminders of major research papers or exams that are coming up in a couple weeks. Such "refreshers" are a great way to keep students continually focused on coursework and learning.

- **Write down specific and routine times for sleeping and eating.** I find the most successful students and professionals usually eat meals at regular times and sleep the same hours every day, including weekends. Now, I understand college students think they don't need such routines. In reality, such consistency can help a person be better focused and alert in classes and at work.

- **Save space in your daily planner for 6-8 hours of sleep, minimum.** You should be getting eight or more hours of sleep each night, but I'm trying to be realistic here. As for those who argue they need only a couple hours of sleep a night, they're fooling themselves. A lack of sleep will lessen a student's ability to focus and learn in class. Likewise, a lack of sleep can lead to an increased level of stress and, again, a reduced ability to focus and learn. Make certain to get in enough sleep time. You are not as capable and alert with 2 to 4 hours of sleep as you think you are.

- **Schedule times to study for classes.** I find that students that set study times are more likely to actually study and obtain good grades. As with sleeping and eating, if you set up a routine time for studying, you will acclimate to it and more likely study.

- **Record hours for any job you have.** I'm a realist; some students need to work in order to pay for books, classes and food. Set aside time for work so you don't forget to go and end up getting fired. That said, be cautious with the amount of hours you work during the week. From my experience, students that work over fifteen hours a week have a harder time completing coursework and maintaining a good GPA.

- **Set aside time each day to relax.** We all need down time or else we will have increased stress levels and find it hard to concentrate and stay motivated for learning. Whether it's to read a novel, hang out with friends or watch your favorite television show, you need time to relax. Schedule time for it. What happens if you don't? Students who do not take breaks, as with professionals who do not take vacations, will likely struggle to stay motivated for learning. As a result, their grades will suffer and their retention of information will be reduced significantly. Now, this does not mean students should be watching television or going out several hours every day. Be realistic and careful; you need time for studies. There will be more time for watching television and going out after you graduate.

Final Tips for Getting Started

So, we now have a foundation from which to begin. Yet, before I start delving into specific academic success strategies, there are a few more bits of advice I'd like to pass on. First, you need to attend your classes. I understand students get sick or have family emergencies, but students that skip classes on a regular basis usually do not graduate with a degree. Try getting a job without a college degree these days. It's possible, but extremely difficult. I missed three classes total during my undergraduate years. I dare you to beat my attendance record (two of those classes I missed because my professor saw how sick I was and he sent me home)!

Secondly, turn off your cell phone and no texting during classes. Why? Cell phones will distract you and others as will your texting. Besides, it's disrespectful to the class and the professor, and the professor's response may be to fail you on the spot. Oh, by the way, there are professors who will fail a student on the spot for using a cell phone in class. You've been warned!

Third, buy and read your textbooks. Yes, I know it's frustrating and downright rude when professors have you purchase a book and then they never use it during the semester. I also know how ridiculously expensive textbooks are. However, students that try to make it through a semester without a textbook often struggle to learn material and/or get good grades on exams and quizzes. You should always buy and read assigned texts. As for ways to cut costs, look for used copies of your textbooks on the internet or in discount bookstores. The earlier you look for a used text, the more likely you will find one at a decent price. What I recommend to my students/advisees is that they contact a professor as soon as they register for a course and ask what text will be required, which should provide the most amount of time to search out used copies. Some colleges and universities allow students to rent textbooks for a semester, which is something to consider (this often requires a student to have a credit card). Also, many chain bookstores routinely offer coupons to customers that submit an email address. Yes, it's annoying to get an endless amount of email notices, but with some coupons providing upwards of 50% off, the junk mail could be worth it. As for selling back books at the end of the semester, I personally recommend that you keep textbooks related to your major/career path. Those texts may just come in handy for a future class or after you graduate and are working in your chosen profession.

Finally, if you intend to use a laptop for taking notes during class or to use a tape recorder/digital recorder to record lectures, ask for permission from the professor first. It's a matter of respect you owe her/him. By the way, many of us who teach can tell when students are instant messaging friends or accessing the internet. Do you really want to fail a class because you were caught updating your Facebook page?

Chapter 3

Note-taking Strategies

Taking accurate notes only gets you so far in your college career. To get A's in your courses, you must continually study notes to retain the information. Now, as a realist, I recognize that students jam a lot into their schedules and are unlikely to spend hours every day going over their notes. To that end, I advise students to adhere to the following guidelines, which helped me maintain A's and B's throughout my undergraduate years.

- **Sit within the first two rows during class.** It's hard to get distracted when the professor is right in front of you, and it's easier to hear the professor and see what he/she writes on the chalk/white board. Sitting within the first few rows also makes it easier to hear questions and feedback from other students in the class, and such student involvement may be just what you need to better understand the lecture material.

- **Don't sit near friends**. It's great to take a class with a good friend especially when you miss a class and need to get notes or when you want a study partner for tests. However, it's hard to concentrate on lecture material or focus on taking clear, accurate notes when a friend is continually talking your ear off. Let your friends know that during class you will not engage in any discussion not related to course material or part of the acceptable student exchanges during a class environment. Good friends will understand this, and you might just help guide your friend into developing good study habits.

- **Ask your professor to repeat/clarify anything you don't understand or didn't clearly hear.** I know it is not easy to raise your hand in class and ask for clarity. After a lifetime of battling an anxiety disorder, I know too well the fear of looking "stupid" or "like an idiot" and have lost countless, easy points on numerous tests over the years simply because I didn't ask a professor to repeat or clarify something during a lecture. First, let me tell you an important truth: any question you raise is likely the same question most of the other students in class have; the other students are just afraid to ask the question. Asking a question is what dedicated learners do, and in asking a question such students usually are helping out everyone else. Did you ever feel relief because someone asked a question you had but were unwilling to ask? It happens a lot. Asking a question is a sign of intelligence and courage. As a professor, I encourage my students to ask me questions immediately, because later material usually builds on topics discussed at the beginning of class. If you struggle like I did to speak up in class, ask the professor for clarity after class or during her/his office hours.

- **Develop a system of shorthand for notes to quicken your recording of professor's lecture.** Let's face it, some professors ramble on during lectures; I'm guilty of this, I know. Without the aid of a recording device, how does a student possibly write down all important information presented during a class? Using a system of shorthand can make all the difference. Shorthand is a system of symbols a person develops, symbols that refer to words. For example, instead of writing *and* or *plus*, write down the symbol '+'. Now, admittedly this example only saves a student a few seconds. However, when developing and using a shorthand system, those few extra seconds saved begin to add up. Thanks to the advent or instant messaging and now text messaging, most people are well versed in using shorthand, which makes this even easier to implement.

Examples:

Symbol	In Place Of
+	Plus
-	Minus or subtract
X	Times or Except
PPL	People
%	Percent
<	Less Than
>	Greater Than
&	And
ENV	Environment
∴	Therefore

- **Any terms, individuals or other material your professor spends a lot of time discussing you should pay careful attention to.** Many students struggle with identifying what are the important notes or, in other words, the notes relevant to upcoming test questions. Admittedly, students have a much easier time determining what's important AFTER the first test. But, what about determining the important lecture material for the first test? Fortunately, there are a number of indicators that can help students isolate important lecture discussions from the unconnected tangents professors tend to go off on. First, professors, myself included, often repeat important information or change the tone/pace of their voice when covering something important. Second, we professors tend to draw diagrams or post an image on a PowerPoint slide of important individuals or objects that students will need to know for a test. Third, if a professor writes down a name or phrase on a chalkboard or whiteboard and then underlines it, that's usually a good indication those particular notes will ultimately be translated into a quiz or test question. In all the above instances, you should write down the corresponding information in you notebook.

- **Write down terms and people from textbooks that pop up in lectures.** Students should read textbook material before it is discussed in class if possible. In the event you successfully do this, pay attention for words, events or individuals mentioned in lectures which also were mentioned in textbook chapters. Textbooks are primarily used to reinforce and clarify key topics, which ultimately show up as test questions. So, when such repetition occurs, write down the information repeated.

- **Write down information in lectures that corresponds to topics listed on the syllabus.** For many professors, a syllabus becomes an outline for structuring the entire semester. Consequently, we write down people, events, theories or other topics that are of primary importance to the courses we teach. If a syllabus indicates that the topic of discussion for a given day will be on George Washington, it behooves students to take notes on anything or anybody discussed in class that day that is connected to George Washington.

- **Use margins of notebook paper to add additional points or to write down questions you have regarding material and wish to ask a tutor or the professor to clarify.** One of the greatest advances with regards to study techniques was the Cornell note-taking system developed by Cornell professor Dr. Walter Pauk. Over the last twenty years, I have heard a number of interpretations of this note-taking system and do not plan to argue the pros and cons of the variations here. Instead, I just wanted to give students quick insight into some of the ways I utilized this system. First, using regular notebook paper, draw two lines across the sheet of paper, the first a vertical line to separate the left 1/3 of the page from the right 2/3 portion. Then, draw a horizontal line separating the bottom 6 to 7 lines from the top portion of the page. Doing this will provide three separate sections for writing notes, questions and other important information. The right side of the page is what students should use to record notes from lectures. Remember, as discussed earlier, use a shorthand system for writing notes to make the most use of the space provided. The left-hand column, meanwhile, is a section to write down questions you may have about the material, questions you should then seek clarification of via the professor or the course textbook. This left-hand column also is a place to write terms or the names of people or events which your professor deems important (i.e. the professor spends considerable time on the term or underlines the term on the chalkboard/whiteboard or on a PowerPoint slide). The final section along the bottom is a space that is reserved for after class. As soon as possible, after class, students should review the notes they took during class, which includes looking over notes in both the left and right-hand columns. Then, in the bottom space, summarize the notes from the lines above. This is a great space to write down what the student perceives would be hypothetical test questions based on the written notes.

		Notes:
O	Key Terms	
O		
O	Summary	

- **Rewrite notes when necessary and as soon as possible.** My handwriting has always been awful to say the least. During class, it was always hard for me to keep up with the professor, so my hand would write at a bazillion words a minute (or at least you would easily assume that after seeing my handwriting skills).

Sloppy doesn't even begin to cover how atrocious my writing was. Then, at times when I failed to read over my notes after class or within twenty-four hours, I would go to study and find that I could not read what I actually wrote in my notebook! Funny thing is, I'm sure most students find themselves in a similar situation at one time or another. What's the solution? After class (or as soon after as possible), read over the notes you took. If you have trouble deciphering anything you wrote, rewrite it as soon as possible! Why! Because, the more time you wait to rewrite the notes, the more likely the corresponding information will become lost as far as your memory is concerned. As an aside, rewriting notes is a nice way to study. While it doesn't make you a friend of trees, rewriting notes will reinforce what you read and learned in class. For my most difficult classes, I would rewrite notes each night, and I found doing so made it easier for me to determine what made sense to me and what information I needed to ask the professor or a tutor to clarify for me.

- **Reducing note-taking-induced stress.** Let's face it, taking notes is stressful! I mean, think of all the questions that run through your mind before, during and after you take notes. *Did I write down the important information? Did I forget to write down an important name? Is one of those tangents the professor went off on important and should I have written it down?* And for those who skip class and then borrow notes from a classmate: *did they write down all the crucial information?* You see what I mean? Taking notes is stressful! Well, here's some tips for reducing that stress. First, accept that you will NEVER be able to write down everything important said by a professor! You're Human; accept that and move on. It's okay that you are not perfect at note-taking, because no one is! Second, to increase the likelihood that you will get most of the important information, partner up with a classmate. Set time aside each week to discuss class lectures and notes. These group study sessions will help increase your chances of academic success as well as reduce your stressing over notes. Lastly, ask your professor for feedback on your notes. You'd be amazed at how many professors will sit down and glance over a student's notebooks to see if the student is recording the pertinent information. Worst case scenario, the professor won't look over your notes. More often than not, your professor will glance over your notes and point out important things you missed. The professor may just also point out items in the notes that are good candidates for test questions. Try one or all of these techniques, and you will soon find that your note-taking stress fades into nothing.

Final Tips for Taking Notes: Retaining the Information

It's not enough to write down the notes, because you'll forget the information quickly if you don't take time to review your notes. When should you begin the review process? Students should review notes immediately after class or as soon as their schedule permits (in the event a student has another class or work immediately after a class). Specifically, you should look over the notes taken that day, taking time to rewrite any sentences or words that are difficult to read, an effort you'll appreciate when you revisit notes in preparation for tests. Students should spend a minimum of fifteen to twenty minutes on this task. If there is any material you don't understand, ask your professor or a tutor for clarification as soon as possible. That's the first step towards retaining the information in your notes.

Once you get home or to your dorm room, take another twenty minutes in the evening to read over your notes. If you had three classes that day, that means you need to spend twenty minutes per class to scan notes. What I additionally encourage my students/advisees/tutees to do is to spend time Saturday going over the past week's notes for each class and Sunday reviewing all notes taken since the last exam (do this for each class). Yes, I understand students have a lot of other things going on (reading text material, working on research papers, hanging out with friends, eating, sleeping, etc). That said, students need to treat their college career as a full-time job, which means investing time in studying notes. It may help to know that every semester I followed this advice resulted in a semester GPA of 3.5 or higher. Also, I found that after struggling to get into this review habit, it became a routine that was simple to complete and made it easier to prepare for exams. As an extra bonus, this method of reviewing helped to substantially DECREASE my test anxiety later on in the semester, because I was more comfortable with the material and more confident I understood the information covered.

- **Special notes to remember:** During class time, a student's focus needs to be on the lecture/professor's presentation. Talking, texting, passing notes and staring out a window are actions that will make it difficult for a student to retain information. Additionally, getting caught doing any of these actions could get you kicked out of the class, permanently. Think about it! You are paying to be in that class, in some cases thousands of dollars for one course. Do you really want to waste that much money, money you have to pay back if you took out a loan? Go to class and give your professor your undivided attention. It's the smart and respectful thing to do.

Chapter 4

Class Participation Do's and Don'ts

Class participation, or a lack thereof, often plays a significant role in a student's comprehension of course material and subsequent performance on quizzes and tests. Students that ask questions whenever they don't understand material or generate discussion during class generally obtain a better understanding of course material and higher grades on class assessments. What about students that rarely ask questions or participate? They usually struggle to pass courses let alone get A's or B's.

In the last section, I covered note-taking strategies that help students retain and organize lecture material. That advice won't help a student who is routinely skipping classes or students who are distracted during classes. Likewise, what about students who don't understand part of a class lecture and yet fail to ask for clarification? Understanding will not magically occur during a test, which means these effectively absent students will probably do poorly if not fail the class outright without asking for clarification. Consequently, participating in class discussions and asking questions is essential for college students who wish to achieve academic success. The question is how do students effectively participate?

As someone who struggled with public speaking, I know speaking up in class and contributing to a discussion is extremely difficult. Therefore, before listing some important Do's and Don'ts related to participation, I wanted to offer advice on how students should gradually increase their participation until reaching some sort of comfort zone with class participation.

First, accept the responsibility of being an active participant in class as opposed to just an observer. You need to be an active learner to succeed, which includes an obligation to help direct class discussions. Yes, some professors discourage student participation. From my experience as a student, such educators are few and far between. As a professor, I greatly appreciate the input received from my students during class as it helps the class better understand the material while also teaching me better ways to present lectures.

After accepting this potentially overwhelming responsibility, students should effort to show up to class prepared to ask at least one question per class. As an undergraduate and graduate student, I would write down a few questions related to material professors were covering. While my initial goal was to ask one question per class, I eventually worked until I could ask as many questions as I needed to. There were classes where I struggled to ask even one question per week, but I eventually found myself able to start semesters asking multiple questions whenever necessary. Having battled an anxiety disorder my entire life, I appreciate the difficulty of such an endeavor. However, I can't stress enough that participating in class is necessary for success.

Class Participation Do's

- **Go to class.** It's next to impossible to understand course material and, ultimately, succeed in college without actually attending classes. Likewise, students need to be on time and stay for the entire class. Missing even a minute of a lecture could be disastrous for a student's understanding of presented material.

- **Maintain eye-contact with your professor when asking or answering questions.** Aside from showing respect to the professor, maintaining eye contact will lessen the likelihood a professor will not hear a student's question or response.

- **Ask questions as soon as any arise.** For those students who struggle with public speaking, write down questions and then ask the professor after class or during her/his office hours for clarification. Failure to ask questions may lead a student to forget about material until the middle of the next test when a relevant question surfaces.

- **Attempt to participate during every class.** Students who continually participate generally are better prepared for tests and quizzes, which are often based solely on class lectures. In situations where class participation contributes to a student's final class grade, asking even one or two questions per class may help assure maximum participation points.

Class Participation Don'ts

- **Don't text or visit social networking websites during class.** First, if a student spends time updating a Facebook page, he/she will likely miss important points presented in a class lecture. Second, in classes where professors consider class participation when calculating final grades, such disrespectful behavior could significantly hurt a student's final grade or even lead to expulsion from class, and for the record, it's usually easy to spot students who are texting or otherwise occupied on a laptop. You've been warned!

- **Don't cutoff others while they are speaking.** Fellow students may provide insight that helps others understand lecture material. Consequently, any interruption may restrict valuable feedback from others. Additionally, such behavior may discourage other students from contributing valuable points in future classes. If you have a question to ask or a point to make, raise your hand and wait to speak until the professor permits you to.

- **Don't use class discussion as outlet for personal causes.** Students are certainly entitled to their opinions. However, shifting focus of a class discussion away from a professor's point or objective could limit time for relevant questions, which may hurt students' performance on tests and quizzes.

- **Don't criticize or demean others during class discussion.** Such disrespectful behavior needlessly hurts others and distracts class from important information. Remember, every college student has the right to be heard and the right to ask questions, and asking questions is the way to gain knowledge. Understanding something that someone else fails to understand doesn't make you any smarter as a whole; you just have knowledge that person lacks. In all likelihood, every person you meet knows something you don't. By the way, showing such disrespect towards other students may get you removed from class.

*** In the event a student is extremely anxious during class and he/she is unable to ask questions before, during or after class because of that fear, the student should speak with a member of the college counseling staff. Counselors can help students confront and overcome such fears. Needing and asking for this help is not something to be ashamed of. Rather, it is a sign of courage to ask for help, and it is something I wish I had done when I was an undergraduate student.

Chapter 5

Reading Strategies That Work

College textbooks can be a bit boring, which is a statement I doubt many college students would dispute. Sure, every once in a while professors assign books that are riveting page-turners, but such instances rarely happen. For me, even subjects I was extremely interested in such as history and science made for some long nights staring at text that seemed lifeless. The thing is, students have to read because tests, quizzes and homework assignments often pull information directly from course textbooks. In some instances, students will get a professor who talks endlessly about trivial topics only to test strictly on material from the textbook, material which the professor never actually covered in class lectures. Consequently, if you don't read, you won't pass. To that end, I listed the reading strategies that helped me and continually help my advisees/students to get through textbook material while retaining the most information possible.

Read, Read, Read

I'm always amazed at the students who return textbooks at the end of the year (after having paid over $100 dollars per text) and the shrink wrap is still covering the books. To add insult to injury, those students often get about $20 for each book they sell back, if they are lucky. Let's put aside the issue that these students just lost $80. From my experience as a tutor, a professor and an advisor, the students in this situation rarely succeed in college courses. You cannot retain textbook information if you don't read the book! Additionally, professors often create test questions directly from text in course books. So, if you don't read the text, you're losing out on an easy study technique. Reading college textbooks is essential if a student wants to successfully complete coursework and earn a degree. In other words; read, read, read! Having said that, let's address the problems with textbooks in order to identify methods for reading textbooks without too much trouble. The major problems I encountered with my textbooks were that:

1) Chapters can be long, requiring hours just to read one chapter.

2) It's hard to retain information when there is so much reading to do.

3) Many of the words used in textbooks are not well defined, which makes it difficult to understand readings.

4) It's often necessary to reread entire chapters in order to master the material covered in the text.

5) **Did I mention that textbook material can be really, really boring!**

I'm sure every student has a number of added problems he or she faces when it comes to reading a textbook and retaining presented material. However, the above list covers the major concerns that many students face. I tackled these same problems with textbooks. How did I get through the chapters and retain the information? How did I reduce the need to reread textbook chapters when it came time to study for exams? It was a series of steps I took that addressed all these concerns, which included reading chapters over a period of time, looking up unfamiliar words in a dictionary as I read, and summarizing textbook material as I read.

Reading Periods

Reading a chapter in one sitting is a daunting task, particularly when the text material is rather dry and uninspiring. What did I do to get through reading my textbooks? I used to read textbook chapters over a period of several hours. Admittedly, some textbook chapters are longer (and more boring) than others you'll have to read, but the following approach worked best for me.

Step 1: Start early. Not only is it painful trying to read a month's worth of reading within the days before an exam, it's also relatively useless. Why? Because it will be difficult for your brain to analyze, comprehend and RETAIN that much information in such a limited amount of time. What is the upside of beginning to read materials early? You will limit the amount of reading you need to get done each week. I encourage all students to start reading textbook chapters as soon as possible, beginning the first week of classes. Get reading into your daily schedule immediately so that you won't be tempted to delay reading textbook chapters until right before a test.

Step 2: Read in set time increments. For many students, reading textbooks is tedious, and therefore it is easy to become distracted if a student doesn't put in place a time limit for her/his reading sessions. Thirty to forty minutes worked for me. I would sit down and read approximately half a chapter in about thirty minutes and then rest my eyes and relax for about ten minutes. Then, I would read for another thirty to forty minutes in that text and call it a day for that course/textbook. Notice I didn't say I stopped reading entirely? I found that reading material for one class longer than an hour made it difficult for me to concentrate and retain the information (as well as any in formation I read in other textbooks). Jumping to another subject/textbook helped to enliven my studies up a bit.

- Regarding the ten-minute break I suggested? Don't use the break to watch television, play a computer game or check your email. Why? Because your attention will drift and you'll be less likely to regain your focus on the textbook material if you even return to reading at all.

Word Search 101

How does a student analyze and comprehend a textbook passage when he or she doesn't understand what a word in the passage means? The answer is the student won't fully comprehend the passage. Sure, a student may get the gist of the passage, but total understanding will be hard to obtain and lead to a student misunderstanding future textbook passages. This is where that collegiate dictionary I recommended you get comes into play. If you come across a word you don't know the meaning of, look it up. If the word is not in your dictionary (sometimes this will happen) look the word up online or in an unabridged dictionary. Why is this so important? It's important because understanding the word will help you understand the passage better. Additionally, you will understand future reading better when that word pops up again. Does that seem like wasted effort on your part? It's not. In fact, it's exactly what a dedicated and successful college student would do. By the way, when looking up words online, be careful of the website you obtain a definition from. Look for definitions from

'.edu' sites or from professional websites related to the subject matter. For instance, when looking up a definition for a Biology class, a personal blog will likely be less reliable than a college or university's Biology Department webpage.

Text Summaries

Read a chapter in any of your textbooks and then try to describe in detail what the chapter was about. Not an easy thing to do is it? After reading paragraph upon paragraph for any length of time, a reader's ability to recall the information is going to be negligible at best. How does a student contend with this reality? For me and many of my students, summarizing textbook passages while reading helps students retain and recall information. What that entails is the following:

- **Outline chapters as you read, writing down section titles to separate notes.** This breakdown of textbook sections will help direct your study efforts later (see example).

- **Consider and rewrite section titles as a question (underneath section title in your outline) and write a summary of the textbook section so that it answers the question.** Doing so will help you identify what is the importance of the passage.

- **Write down any bold-faced or italicized words found in each section and their associated definitions.** Such font styles often note important terms you need to know for tests.

- **Write down any names, events or dates you find in text that relate to

class lectures you recall. Such connections between class discussions and textbook passages often point towards material likely to be covered on tests.

- **Underline in pencil any words, or phrases or sentences you consider important (any terms or ideas discussed in class should be underlined when they appear in the class textbook).** Later, when reviewing textbook passages in preparation for tests, these marks will help direct your attention towards crucial information.

- **Avoid highlighting.** Why? Highlighting is meant to call attention to/isolate material that appears important so that in the future the student can focus study time on fewer areas of the text. What I have found is that students will highlight entire pages. So much for the highlighting isolating a few important points. Additionally, if you underline in pencil, you can erase the pencil marks and possibly get back more money when you sell a book back to the college bookstore.

- **Write down any questions you have (in pencil) in the margins of the book.** You should then ask your professor about those questions as soon as possible. This will clarify material and help in retaining and recalling text information. Those notes in the margins will also serve to direct your attention to book sections you need to spend more time on for clarification.

- **Use your outline of textbook chapters as a study guide for tests and quizzes.** This is one of the great benefits of outlining chapters in your textbooks; the outlines serve as a guide to important information you'll likely be tested on.

Final Reading Tips

The above tips regarding Reading assignments should provide students with a guidebook for successfully understanding and retaining information contained within textbooks. In conclusion, there are a few more bits of information I suggest students consider regarding reading assignments. First, when encountering any material that is hard to understand, ask the course professor or a tutor to decode/explain the text. It's especially important to get the professor's feedback in these instances because he/she will be able to provide an interpretation of the text from her/his eyes/perspective.

Also, if a textbook includes questions to consider at the end of chapters, attempt to answer the questions. If you can't answer the questions you probably did not grasp the material completely. It's important to also note that professors sometimes use the questions presented in textbooks as actual test questions. Finally, if the publisher created web-based resources for the textbook (sample quizzes, vocabulary lists, chapter summaries, etc.), take the time to utilize those resources. At a basic level, if a student spent over $100 for a textbook, he or she should get the most for their money. More importantly, these resources can help clarify textbook material. By the way, publishers often seek input from professors (including me) in designing/creating online support material. Consequently, there is a likelihood your professor may use the support material to create quiz and test questions. Did I also mention that most of the available resources are free of charge?

A final bit of advice stems from what I learned from my parents. In many respects, my parents helped me improve my reading comprehension abilities more than any professor or teacher did. What's Mom and Dad's secret? They encouraged me to read novels, magazines, newspapers and other material as soon as I could read. Way before students had summer reading lists, my parents required me to spend part of my summers reading (and they questioned me to make certain I was actually reading and retaining information). To reinforce their position on reading, both my parents seemed to always be reading when they had a free moment. This family reading regimen kept my reading skills sharp and my comprehension and retention of read material high. By getting into a similar habit of reading for pleasure, students will likely increase their ability to read through and understand reading required for courses. From my experience, avid readers have an easier time completing reading assignments and, ultimately, are more successful in college and life.

***Sample Chapter Outline of This Chapter

I. Reading Strategies That Work

The following reading strategies are ways to get through textbook readings retaining as much information as possible.

II. *Read* [Why do students need to Read? What happens if students don't?]

To succeed and retain as much information as possible, a college student has to actually read the textbooks assigned to their classes. Failing to read the texts will likely lead to a student failing the class. It's also a waste of money as the student purchased a book, never used it and then sells it back to the bookstore for little money.

III. Reading Periods [What are Reading Periods? How are they set up?]

Reading periods are set times in a student's schedule for reading text material. Spend up to 80 minutes reading (per class) each day (break reading up into two 30-40 minute time periods separated by a 10 minute break.) Start using reading periods as soon as the semester begins.

IV. Wordsearch 101 [What does 'wordsearch' mean? Why is it important?]

'Wordsearch' means students should look up words they don't know in a dictionary as soon as possible (or look up definitions on 'reputable websites'). If you don't, you will not likely understand the rest of the text material.

<u>Unabridged Dictionary</u>: Dictionary that includes all officially recognized words in the English language.

<u>Collegiate Dictionary</u>: Dictionary containing range of words often used in college settings.

V. Text Summaries [What are 'text summaries'? What should they include?]

These are outlines of chapter readings, which provide a study guide for students later on as they prepare for tests/quizzes. Text summaries should include summaries of text sections and lists of definitions for italicized and bold-faced terms. Include names of important events, important people and anything in text that was mentioned in class lectures. Turn text section titles into questions and use the text to answer the questions created.

Chapter 6

Writing an "A" Research Paper

A social science (Anthropology) major, I wrote a lot of research papers. Interestingly enough, whether the paper was a 5-pager, a twenty pager, or my Master's Thesis, the process I used to write my papers remained consistent, and rarely did I obtain a grade lower than an A. My success in writing research papers was founded on a variety of tips I learned through talking to professors or tutors and through experimenting with methods to ultimately see what worked for me. Listed below are the writing strategies that provided me and many of my students the direction to maintain

A's on research papers at both undergraduate and graduate school levels.

- **Start Early!** Students often tell me that they "work better under pressure," which is why they wait until a few days before the due date to start a paper. Not surprising, most of these students fail to obtain A's on their papers. Writing a research paper, regardless of the subject matter, is a relatively relaxed process IF a student starts as early as possible to begin the paper. Think of it this way. Would you rather stay up for 72 hours straight to put together a C or B graded paper, or would you rather spend small chunks of time over a three to six week period to conduct research, write a paper and get it proofread, all on your way to getting an "A"? For the record, I too thought I worked better under pressure, writing research papers in a limited amount of time. When I started giving myself more time, I started getting A's.

- **Generate a Thesis Statement as soon as possible.** The thesis statement is the most important component of your paper. For readers, the thesis statement informs them of what the paper will cover and in what order evidence/data will be presented. For your professor, the thesis statement, provided in the introductory paragraph, lets her/him immediately know if the student truly understood the assignment and the related material. In writing your thesis, ask yourself if the thesis answers questions posed by the assignment. At this point, don't worry about a finalized introductory paragraph; you can take care of that a bit later. After you feel your thesis is strong, have your professor and/or a tutor read over the thesis statement. Keep working on the thesis until it meets your professor's approval. Yes, it may take a bit of time to get the thesis completed. However, since thesis statements help outline the entire paper and provide guidelines for readers and writers alike, it's worth the time invested.

- **Get papers proofread.** I have published short stories, peer-reviewed journal articles and several novels. Yet, as much experience writing as I have, I always have at least a couple typos pop up during the editing process. Always have someone else read over/proofread your papers, because they will likely catch typos you missed. To get the most out of proofreading, have a tutor read your paper out loud to you; it's a great way to improve your writing skills. Also, I recommend asking your professor to read over a paper before the due date. See if the professor will point out inconsistencies, typos, etc. and whether or not the professor will estimate your grade/allow you to make corrections and resubmit. It's an effort that could help you ensure an A.

- **Properly cite sources.** Whether you use a direct quote or you paraphrase what an author wrote, you must cite where you obtained information that is not "Common Knowledge." How do you determine what is common knowledge? How do you know when a citation is absolutely necessary? Ask your professor directly about information prior to turning in the paper. He or she will be able to let you know if you need to cite. My personal standpoint is that if a writer is uncertain whether or not to provide a citation, he or she should provide a citation (better safe than sorry). Why is this so important? Using someone else's research/ideas to substantiate arguments in a research paper without citing is considered theft of an idea (Plagiarism). At best, students that plagiarize fail the paper. Worst case scenario? A student could be expelled from the college. As for how to cite properly, first determine which citation style your professor prefers (Chicago, MLA, APA, etc.). Then follow current rules for that citation style (this information can be found online or a student can see a writing tutor or a librarian for assistance).

Special Note on Citations: Paraphrasing Vs. Quoting

Many students come to college with little or no experience citing sources used in research papers. Therefore, I thought I would use a little space to address one of the bigger problems I've noticed with freshmen. The problem in question is that many students confuse paraphrasing and quoting or, more specifically, which method of presenting others' ideas requires an actual citation? The answer is BOTH techniques still require a citation.

In the following examples, an analysis is made of the same passage from a novel. Notice that in both instances that a citation referring to where the material was obtained is included at the end. As for the quote, most students understand the need for the citation, because the author's words are being used exactly as written. Why is the citation needed in the paraphrasing example? Because, even though the author's words are not replicated exactly, word for word, the essence/uniqueness of the passage is still used (and my novel can't really be considered common knowledge). Paraphrasing, putting someone else's statement in your own words, is a difficult concept/strategy to learn and employ in research papers. To that end, I strongly recommend that you always have a professor or tutor help you determine whether or not you are 'paraphrasing' accurately. Once again, better safe than sorry.

Sample 1: Quote

As evidenced by passages in the novel PEOPLE OF THE SWORD, author Neil O'Donnell relies on interaction between characters and 'nature' to detail settings, as seen in the following passage:

"The full moon appeared through a gap in the gathering clouds and cast a soft, pale light over him and the surrounding landscape. Algren closed his eyes and listened to the branches knocked about by the mounting wind while tears began to flow from his puffy and reddened eyes." (O'Donnell 2009: 2).

Sample 2: Paraphrase

As evidenced by passages in the novel PEOPLE OF THE SWORD, author Neil O'Donnell relies on interaction between characters and 'nature' to detail settings. ***O'Donnell's use of this technique appeared right at the outset of the novel when the author depicts the druid chieftain, Algren, meandering through a forest and embracing the moonlight and growing wind (O'Donnell 2009: 2).***

Conducting Research

Conducting research for a college paper is a long process usually requiring weeks of hard work and dedicated reading. Consequently, students who try to complete a research paper over a long weekend will unlikely obtain a grade above a 'C' given the time that should be spent researching. In this second edition, I have here added some tips to get students better prepared for conducting such research.

Before providing tips, however, I want to stress the importance of familiarizing oneself with her/his college library. Accept the fact that the library remains the greatest research tool for college students. Sure, students can access a lot of research databases online through their library's website such as JSTOR, ERIC and EBSCOhost. However, physical copies of journals, books and magazines can be examined first hand at the library whereas articles often cannot be read online (if a student's library does not have a subscription to a journal, all a student would be able to do is obtain an article's title and maybe read an abstract for the article). Consequently, I encourage students to become familiar with the layout of their campus library.

Find out where the hard copies of journals are kept, including where additions older than ten years old are stored. Get familiar where published books relevant to your major are located as majors often have their own section for relevant books. While you are at it, look for a comfortable location to study nearby; look for a comfortable study curl or office space reserved for student use. All these steps are worth the time. Why? First, if you dorm, the library can provide solitude especially when your dorm and roommate are not so quiet. That's just the beginning, however.

   Let's say your college's computer network crashes, a reality that WILL happen multiple times each semester. What do you do in those instances? Sure, you could surf the Web and find information. However, without access to journal databases like JSTOR, you will struggle to access journal articles (professors rarely allow just any old blog or Web article to suffice for papers). In such instances, being able to search the hard copies your library has in its collections is a huge benefit. Furthermore, the books in your library may be available online for free viewing. However, books you'll likely use as source materials for papers will be expensive if you attempt to purchase digital copies (most books will not be free to view online, at least not books typically used by students for research papers). Again, knowing the layout of your library and where books for different subjects are will save you time and make it easier to conduct research for any immediate paper as well as for future research papers.

Now, as to conducting actual research, listed here are steps I generally take for researching a subject. Yes, these techniques were what I employed as an undergraduate. That said, as a professional anthropologist, conducting research remains a part of my daily life. What's more, for students who don't pursue careers heavily involved in research, there are other areas of life where strong research skills make a difference. Becoming an informed voter, investigating job markets, selecting a home with a good school system for children, and finding the best investment opportunities all involve significant research. Hence, these tips are transferable to real life situations. In other words, pay attention to the following research tips.

- **Start early and get continual feedback from your professor.** This is a repeat of my earlier comments, particularly getting guidance from a professor. Students often start off in the right direction on a research paper. Unfortunately, little missteps often taken by students can eventually snowball into a major mistake in research. Keeping your professor in the loop and starting research as soon as possible allows more time for correcting your research direction. Believe me, because I know from experience, it's hard to redo research when you learn of your missteps days before the paper is due.

- **Use a database search engine to research your topic.** Most college and university libraries have developed their own search engine, which students can often reach online from their home or dorm room. Many of these search engines will list relevant books and articles at the top of any generated list. From there, start reading/skimming the top suggested articles or books to see if the information is relevant. Keep reading and investigating until you have found five to ten references that hold promise.

- **Carefully examine bibliographies and/or 'References Cited' pages from useful sources.** Once you have five to ten good sources of information, examine each source's list of references. You will likely find a number of books and articles used by the authors that appear relevant to your topic. Record the titles of the articles/books and relevant periodicals and go review them. You will likely find a great many sources of information this way and ultimately save yourself days or even weeks of research time.

- **Ask your professor for book/article suggestions.** Your professors have completed years of research themselves and have likely investigated the topic you are researching. Consequently, a professor may be able to recommend a good book or journal article for you to read for your project. It's worth taking the couple minutes to ask. Aside from your professor, scan the biographies of professors listed on your campus website and look for professors whose specialties match your research. These are additional individuals you should consider asking for direction from.

- **Look at books on shelves nearby to good sources you find.** I spent a lot of time studying cultures from around the world. What I quickly learned is that if I wanted to find additional books on a given culture, all I generally had to do was scan bookshelves above and below any good reference book to find additional resources that pertained to my current research.

Chapter 7

Test Preparations & Success

Test preparation doesn't begin a day or a week before the test takes place (unless, of course, a student is aiming for low or failing grades). Students should start preparing for tests right from the start of the semester (including final exams). To that end, adhering to the academic advice provided in the earlier chapters of this book will help students in their understanding of material and preparations for tests. Advice presented here is meant to augment students' understanding of material to optimize comprehension of course material and preparation for the tests and quizzes that may come along.

- **Show up to class.** You'd think this was an obvious step, but large numbers of students still miss many classes during their college career. How can you learn the information without attending class? Students believe it's possible, but I find it rare when a student who misses a lot of classes maintains A's in her/his classes.

- **Read your books.** Yes, we covered this earlier, but it's worth mentioning again. Failure to read assigned textbook chapters may hinder a student's comprehension of course material. Since many professors create tests based solely on textbook material, not reading could lead a student to failure.

- **Use flash cards.** I almost feel as if students consider flash cards to be an educational tool for children in elementary school, because many times I recommend the use of flash cards, students seemed resistant to the idea. Yet, as a professional tutor, I find that most college students that maintain A's in their classes are using flash cards to some extent. Flash cards are a useful and smart tool to utilize regardless of a student's age. Don't have the money to buy index cards? Just cut up paper into a uniform size (3" x 5"), which is a cost effective way of making flash cards that are just as effective. What information should be included on flash cards? Definitions, equations, math formulas, charts and important individuals and any related accomplishments.

- **Ask a Tutor or the Professor to explain material you don't understand.** Again, I realize we already covered this.

However, waiting until days or even a week before a test to ask for assistance may lower a student's chances to understand the material. What if the professor or your tutor is not available days before the test? What if future material builds on information you failed to understand at the beginning of the semester? Ask for assistance from professors and tutors early on and you will lessen the likelihood of such dilemmas.

- **Music Courses: listen to music early on.** For students taking Music classes, where exams often requiring identifying music selections on tests, start listening to the music on your own immediately after a musical composition is introduced in class. I recommend that students try to visualize a scene from a movie the music reminds them of; it will help in remembering the music. I mention music courses specifically, because students all too often wait until days before tests to begin listening to/reviewing assigned musical selections. **DON'T MAKE THIS MISTAKE.**

- **Generate your own practice quizzes and tests.** Take time to create multiple choice and/or essay questions, acting as if you were in charge of making the test. You can ask your professor or a tutor for guidance (always inform your professor of such efforts prior to creating sample questions – your professor may provide good direction on how to proceed or even provide sample tests). What should you incorporate into your questions? Any material that is repeated in class lectures and textbook readings, information already placed on your flash cards, and/or material from quizzes/earlier tests.

- **Create your own study guide.** Many professors provide their students with study guides for tests. In situations where a professor doesn't provide a study guide, students should create their own. How? Generate a list of terms discussed in lectures or in textbooks as well as a list of people, dates or events covered in class. Students should also write down any questions from quizzes or textbook chapters. Lastly, students should ask their professor to look over the study guide and offer feedback. The professor might just identify material that should be on the study guide, which the student neglected to include.

- **Confront Test Anxiety.** For students who become anxious or nervous during tests, to the point it negatively affects their performance, speak with your college's counseling center staff about ways to defeat Test Anxiety. There are many ways to learn to cope with this type of stress, and doing so can help a student improve their test performance significantly. I didn't deal with my Test Anxiety until I was an upperclassman. I regret waiting because my grades suffered. Please learn from my mistake and seek assistance.

Creating Your Own Sample Test Questions

I help students prepare for quizzes and tests weekly in my capacity as a professional tutor. After over two decades of providing such assistance, I still find that students who generate their own sample tests and quizzes to study from excel the most. Every semester it happens. A student stops by my office and informs me he/she needs assistance preparing for an important test or quiz. After recommending the student complete all readings and create flash cards for important people or terms presented in class or textbooks, I ask if the student considered developing sample questions to study from. My query is often met with a quizzical look followed by the student asking me what I meant. Here is the general explanation I then provide. By the time students are in college, they have completed an array of test and quiz formats ranging from multiple choice exams to essay exams. Bring that experience to study sessions. First, ask professors what format test questions will be presented in (multiple choice, true/false, essay, matching, etc.). From there go through class notes and textbook readings and jot down terms or names that repeatedly appear throughout course material. In my experience, tests and quizzes usually cover people and topics repeated in both lectures and textbook readings. From there, start generating questions related to the important class material while keeping the following in mind.

- **Mix it up with regards to question formats.** Just because the test will be entirely in multiple choice question format doesn't mean a student can't develop a few sample essay questions to study from. Quite frankly, using a variety of question formats will help her/him be better prepared for trick questions professors like to use.

- **Work with a group of classmates to develop questions.** Such a collaborative effort could help students isolate main points of lectures and textbook chapters. Think about it this way, you might not notice an important topic or term that another student realizes as important. Working together, it is less likely an important term will be missed by you and any study partners.

- **Ask a tutor to assist in selecting important topics and creating sample questions.** Tutors often have experience proctoring exams. If you're lucky, the tutor you work with may have even taken the same class with the same professor, which means he/she is likely familiar with the professor's teaching/testing style. Such input can help a student isolate critical terms while also generating sample questions that greatly resemble those that end up on a test or quiz.

- **Ask professor to go over sample questions you develop.** Many professors like to assist students in such endeavors by offering suggestions of topics students should cover on their practice tests. In some cases, professors may even point out questions students don't need to be concerned about, which will help in isolating truly important people and concepts students need to concentrate on.

- **Check textbooks for sample questions.** Many textbooks list important terms, people and concepts at the end of each chapter. Additionally, some texts provide questions, at the beginning of a chapter, for students to consider while reading the chapter. Use any such resources to assist in generating sample test and quiz questions, because they highlight key terms likely to pop up on class assessments.

- **Check for online resources that could provide sample tests or quizzes.** Many textbooks now have associated websites and online material. Check the book's index or the publisher's website to see if such resources exist and utilize them. Let's face it, after spending over $100 for a book, students might as well get their money's worth. As an added bonus, the questions posted online may serve as a template for the test developed by the professor. How effective is this study technique? I get asked that a lot. Usually, at least with those who follow through on this advice, the students stop by after a test or quiz and marvel over how many questions were similar to the sample questions they created. As for the end result, I find that most of my students ultimately receive high grades (A's and B's) when they generate sample questions. Is such a strategy time consuming? You bet. Is it worth the time invested? Well, speaking for myself, it was worth every minute.

Chapter 8

Organizing Effective Study Groups

One of the greatest academic tools in a college student's arsenal is the 'Study Group'. Unfortunately, a study group can just as easily become a hindrance to a student and lead even the best student to academic failure. A normal student reaction to receiving a low or failing test grade is to immediately form a study group with friends in the class. Intent on improving on the next test, the study group participants schedule weekly meetings to go over material covered in lectures and to discuss readings from textbooks and/or journal articles. In general, I think most professors, academic advisors and tutors would say that's a good plan of action. Yet, certain precautions need to be taken to ensure study group participation leads to success. To clarify, consider the following scenario:

Harry receives a 'D' on an Algebra test and fears he will fail the course unless he studies harder. To avoid obtaining future low grades, Harry sets up a study group with four 'C' average classmates, each of whom received low or failing grades on the test. Harry and each member of the study group complete all future assignments and read all corresponding textbook chapters. They then diligently meet a couple times each week in preparation for the ensuing test. Unfortunately, when they take the next test, each of them fails it.

What do you think went wrong? Why did Harry and the other members of his study group do so poorly? Why didn't attending a study group help them do better on the next test? Study groups often prove ineffective when used by college students for the first time. Unfortunately, students in Harry's position often resist future study group participation believing that study groups are a waste of time. What mistakes did Harry and his friends make? First of all, every member of Harry's study group did poorly on the first test. How can they collectively tackle the information when they are all struggling?

Yes, there are instances when such collaboration works. From my experience, when study groups consist entirely of students struggling in the class, most participants do not improve their performance on future tests and, more importantly, continue struggling to understand course material. In this example, Harry and his friends should have invited students that were doing well in the class to join the study group. At least one of a study group's members should be doing well in the course, though preferably two or more study group participants should have an A or B average. That way, the study group has a greater chance of collectively clarifying course material for all participants. In the event that everyone is struggling in the course or none of the academically strong students agree to participate with a study group, ask the professor or a tutor to join the study group. Many professors will join study groups to help students better understand course material. If the professor or tutor you approach does not have time to join the study group, ask her or him for a referral to another professor or tutor who can help. Such action can lead to the development of a successful study group, but it is not the only step to consider.

The second major mistake that Harry and his friends made was in the length of time waited before setting up a study group. Admittedly, students often have no clue they truly don't understand course material until receiving a low or failing grade on the first test. I found myself in this position on a couple occasions as an undergraduate student. That said, students often walk into the first class of a semester knowing which classes are going to be tough. That first day of class is the time to begin thinking of setting up a study group. Over the first few days of a semester, students should acquaint themselves with other students in the class and see if anyone would be interested in forming a study group early on. If students sitting nearby are quiet and less than chatty, ask the professor to pass along a study group sign-in sheet for anyone who wants to join your study group. Leave space on the sheet for interested students' names, email addresses and telephone numbers. Then, schedule weekly meetings immediately that work for everyone's schedule.

Example Sign-in Sheet:

Study Group for Professor O'Donnell's Class

Name	Phone	Email	Days/Times Available

In the event that student schedules conflict, consider rotating times the study group meets or form more than one group. The important thing is to make certain there are study groups that can meet at times you are available. Otherwise, you'll find yourself managing a study group without being able to participate.

This advice aside, consider the following tips to increase the effectiveness of a study group:

- **Set guidelines for study group participation.** Include a list of expectations including that participants keep up on reading and attend classes. Every student should do her/his share of the work load which includes bringing course material and reading assigned text chapters. Additionally, all students should be expected to attend class regularly.

- **Ask professor for study guides to help study group focus on important information.** Additionally, students should all generate their own list of important topics to discuss as well as a list of questions regarding course material from lectures or textbooks.

- **Find a quiet location on campus to meet.** While meeting at one of the member's houses may provide easier access to some members, it is likely that those living in the dorms may find it difficult to travel off campus. Keep in mind that campus libraries often have large rooms that can be reserved by students or professors for study groups.

- **Establish a schedule of chapters and/or topics to discuss at meetings.** A schedule will help study group members keep track of what needs to be done ahead of time and may encourage members to keep up on reading and class attendance. Remember to consider holidays that occur throughout the semester and schedule alternate dates if necessary unless, of course, the study group wants to skip Thanksgiving dinner to go over Algebra.

- **Make allowances for emergencies that arise.** If one of the members misses a week because he or she was sick, be understanding. Any unnecessary animosity in such situations could shatter the study group.

- **Add additional meetings as needed.** If the professor covers a topic that is particularly difficult to comprehend, schedule an extra weekly meeting to specifically address that topic. Likewise, add additional study group sessions in preparation for tests and quizzes.

Chapter 9

Utilize Available Support Services

Most college's and universities offer a range of support services to all their students. With over twenty years of experience tutoring and advising college students, I've learned that the students getting A's and B's in their classes are usually utilizing one or more of those support services. Consequently, I advise all students to use services as needed, particularly the following:

- **Tutors.** Asking a tutor for assistance is a smart move to make. I understand it's difficult for a student to admit he or she is struggling with course material. I struggled with that issue and found it hard to ask for tutoring assistance as a freshman. I was ashamed that I couldn't improve my writing skills and figure out Algebra on my own. I finally got the courage to go to Buffalo State College's EOP Tutoring Center where I received tutoring support. What was the result? I successfully completed my algebra class and excelled in my writing. Don't fear what people will think of your utilizing tutoring services, because it's an act of strength and dedication.

- **Peer tutors vs. Professional tutors.** Most tutoring centers have both undergraduates (peer) and professors (professional) tutoring to assist students. Some students prefer to work with tutors their own age, while other students seek the guidance of tutors with an extensive knowledge of the course subject area. Choose the tutor-level you feel most comfortable with. As for the tutors you work with, tutors utilize a wide range of teaching strategies to assist students. If your tutor's strategies aren't working for you, don't give up on tutoring; seek another tutor. The first writing tutor I worked with wasn't able to help me, but my second tutor was exceptional. If I had abandoned hope of finding a writing tutor that could help me after my first time getting tutoring support, I never would have completed my novels and short stories.

- **Ask professors for guidance and support.** Professors know what exactly appears on the tests and are thereby the best resource for students. A no-brainer, right? Then why do only a handful of students speak to their professors over the course of a semester? Students need to consider meeting with professors to go over course material and clarify confusing subject matter. Professors have office hours for a reason! Yet, few students ever go and see professors during their office hours. I know it can be uncomfortable or embarrassing to inform a professor you don't understand course material, but your professor is truly the best source of information and answers. Early on in my undergraduate career, I found it embarrassing to ask questions during class so I met with the professor after class to discuss any problems I had understanding the material. Doing so helped me build up my confidence to speak up during class and showed me that professors usually are eager to help students with course material.

- **Libraries provide information and a quiet place to study.** I am amazed at the amount of students who go through college never having set foot in the college's library. First and foremost, libraries have endless sources of information, which could be vital to a student's understanding of course material. Secondly, libraries usually offer a quiet place for students to work on reading, research papers and any assignments. Take the time as a freshman to explore your campus library. Find a study curl or table and try completing your homework in that setting. Give it an honest chance and I think you'll find the library to be a great atmosphere to study in. At the very least, you'll likely encounter less disturbances than if you'd studied in your dorm room.

- **Seek assistance from librarians.** Librarians are not just staff members who reshelf books. They are HIGHLY trained specialists capable of helping students with locating library resources, learning how to conduct research, writing bibliographies and getting organized.

- **Utilize campus/community computers and transportation services.** Few students have an extra $500 to $1000 for purchasing a laptop computer. I also find few undergraduate or graduate students have the funds to purchase a car and afford the related costs of repairs, insurance and fuel. Since you are spending a fortune on your college education, it's imperative to cut your costs wherever and whenever possible. Yes, laptops are incredible for portability and logging onto the internet just about anywhere. Yet, college campuses often have countless computers available for students to use, free of charge. Likewise, if your college provides internet access, use it. Paying for an outside internet provider could be costly; save your money for NECESSITIES and use your college's internet hub. As for cars, they're great for independence and convenience. Yet, most campuses are within range of public transportation. Some colleges and universities even maintain their own bus lines or provide a free bus pass to all students. OK, I admit it's a pain at times to wait for a bus, which I did throughout my undergraduate years in Buffalo, New York. Yet, doing so saves you from putting mileage on a personal car, paying for gas, or shelling out hundreds of dollars yearly for repairs to your car's brakes, radiator, tires, starter, muffler, and transmission.

Chapter 10

Money Management Basics

Money may seem like a weird issue to bring up in a study skills manual, but there is a lot to be said about the impact money has on student success and stress levels. Between the outrageous price of textbooks to the exorbitant prices for food and dorm supplies in campus bookstores, it's a wonder students have any success at all. Why? It's hard to be successful when you can't afford textbooks for class or you're struggling to afford dinner. What's more, students often put little thought into the debt they accrue as undergraduates. As the average college student ends up with over ten thousand dollars of loan debt alone after graduation, it is vital to consider what students are spending money on and how to save whenever possible to reduce debt. Now, I've always been a bit of a saver, which was a major reason I left my undergraduate college with no debt. What was my secret? How did I pay for tuition, save and still have money to go to dinner with friends periodically. Here are the major steps I took which made it possible.

- **Look for scholarships as soon as possible BEFORE your senior year of high school.** It is never too early to look for scholarships when it comes to preparing for college and there are a lot of little-known scholarships and grants available to students. And, with relatively few students applying for scholarships, a student's odds of getting scholarship money are a bit higher than most people realize. First, start talking with a high school guidance counselor about scholarships and academic grants he or she is familiar with. Ask about large and small scholarships, because a student could amass multiple small scholarships that have the same monetary value as one large scholarship. Additionally, check to see if the city you reside in has any special funding programs for residents attending college such as the Say Yes Programs available in cities including Buffalo and Syracuse, New York. Don't forget to also see if your parent, parents or guardian's employer provides college funds/scholarships for children of employees. Many of these scholarships likely require students to have GPAs higher that C+ (2.5). Be mindful of these requirements and others.

- **Discuss joining a college savings program with your parents.** Programs like

Upromise or SmarterBucks give cash back towards college expenses (sometimes including loans). Simply by shopping with a program's partnering businesses, students will earn cash for college.

- **Try to save money for books throughout your senior year of high school if possible and build an emergency fund of at least $250.** If you don't know already, college textbooks are incredibly expensive. How expensive? Let's just say that having to buy a textbook priced over $200 is by no means a rare occurrence, especially when students are a natural science major. What I suggest is that students build up a 'Textbook Fund' kept in a bank and untouched except for purchasing textbooks. Then, during a student's senior year at high school, put as much money as possible into that account. Keep adding to this fund throughout your college years to make certain your supplies are covered. Then, whatever is left over after you graduate can be applied towards paying off loans or purchasing other necessities. Additionally, have a separate account where you save a minimum of $250 as an emergency fund (the higher the better). Let this fund simply be for emergencies like a plane ticket to go home for an emergency or for food. Frankly, this emergency fund is something students should continue to build up after graduating, because it's always nice to have emergency money reserved for surprises that come along like an unexpected car repair or the need to purchase basic necessities such as prescriptions, food or toilet paper.

- **Consider attending a community college to get an Associate's before transferring to a four year college.** Now, before you bypass this tidbit, please consider what I have to say. Community colleges offer an array of educational programs, particularly Associate's degrees and professional certificates that would allow a graduate to go right into a number of fields immediately, fields which may pay a good salary and offer a variety of career options. Many people, educators included, are hesitant to recognize this, but the fact of the matter is that not every career path requires a Bachelor's or graduate degree. This is especially true of trades such as carpentry or plumbing. Yet, even beyond these career options, students can often attend a community college and then transfer into a four-year college or university. In these instances, the community college students will have most if not all of their general studies taken care of by their Associate's coursework, but they will have paid much less money for the courses and thereby have less dept.

- **Attend public colleges.** Whether you go to a community college, a four year college or a university, public institutions of higher education are most often the best investment a student can make. Generally, state and county colleges are significantly less expensive than private colleges and universities, tuition-wise. "A private college looks better on a resume" you say? Not necessarily. A number of public colleges and universities are world-renowned and carry a lot of weight in the eyes of businesses. In fact, a lot of businesses are collaborating with public institutions and hiring these institutions' graduates after the students complete an internship. The big issue in most cases is that the college or university you attend be ACCREDITED. Many job ads even expressly state that applicants need a degree from an "accredited" college. All this said, you have to look at the individual track records of the colleges you apply to. Does a college have a higher track record of students graduating and ultimately passing national exams or obtaining employment related to the students' degrees? In many cases, public institutions have a similar or better track record than their private competitors. At that point, students should definitely be considering what is the better investment.

- **Get a job.** I worked as an undergraduate and paid for my college on my own. I worked roughly twenty hours a week during semesters and then forty or more during summer breaks. By doing this, I never had to take out a loan while an undergraduate. I went to a public college (Buffalo State College), and every job I've had since graduating was tied into my major (Anthropology). Now, working a job offered benefits beyond money for tuition. I worked in a restaurant where I could eat. I also worked as a tutor during the academic year and as a field archaeologist during summers, all of which provided me good experience for my resume. The key here is that I limited my hours during semesters so that I could focus on my studies. For most students, working more than fifteen hours a week will make it difficult for them to retain course information and do well on exams. Keep this in mind if you decide to work while in college.

- **Save money over breaks.** Students usually are tempted over winter and summer breaks to spend a lot of time hanging out with friends and spending money. Now, while I am all for unwinding over break to avoid academic-burnout, it is important for students to take every opportunity on breaks to work and save money. Even saving $20 to $100 per week can go a long ways to reducing a student's college debt. I know how tempting it is to just party throughout a summer or winter break. Keep in mind though that the effort to work and save over breaks could ultimately reduce your college dept by tens of thousands of dollars, which in turn could mean you will be out of debt from loans in five to ten years versus twenty to thirty years.

- **Buy textbooks and supplies online or at discount stores.** As I have already stated, college bookstores are extremely expensive. To save money, students should make every effort to purchase books online from discount stores, which could save a student several hundred dollars a semester. Students should also look into 'renting' textbooks, which again could save a student hundreds of dollars. Keep in mind that a credit card is often required to rent a book. In addition to books, students should purchase basic supplies like pens and notebooks at discount stores off campus. While not offering as huge a savings as books do, the few dollars here and there saved will add up.

- **Buy food off campus/make your own meals.** Just like the bookstore, college eating establishments charge more for food than if a student simply went to a supermarket and bought food with which to make her/his own meals. This may not be convenient, especially for those living in dorms without a kitchen or kitchenette. Also, some students, often freshmen, are required to pay for a meal-plan. However, if it is at all possible, make your own meals as it will be most likely cheaper and often better suited to your tastes.

- **Live at home.** I know the arguments favoring students dorm for a true college experience. I concede that dorm-life has it's advantages, but there are a number of drawbacks, too, which people often gloss over. If you can live at home and not pay rent, you could save tens of thousands of dollars as an undergraduate. It may not be as convenient to attend campus activities, but the cost savings could be tremendous. Frankly, you could save a lot of money living at home and then just pay for a great trip after graduating and not have a massive amount of debt.

- **Become an RA.** Resident assistants are students who live in the dorms and monitor the other students. These usually paid positions often include a stipend for free housing and free food. Yes, RAs have a lot of responsibilities, and their job is far from easy. However, not having to pay for room and board could equate to a huge amount of savings over time.

- **Invest as much money as you can as soon as you can.** This last one is tricky, because few students have any extra money from my experience. However, if you find yourself with an extra $10 or so, consider depositing it into a savings or retirement account that you do not touch! This is definitely something to discuss with a financial consultant before doing. Yet, if you are able to do this to any extent, you could find interest gathered by this account generating tens of thousands of dollars over the next few decades. Remember, it is never too early to start saving for retirement.

I'm sure you noticed that many of these tips refer to steps to take as high school students to better financially prepare for the expenses that come with college life. Don't let that frustrate you. There is always time to save something and help reduce your ultimate college dept. The big key is to start as soon as possible and keep chipping away at college debt until it's gone.

Chapter 11

Final Advice for Attaining Success

The strategies detailed in this book played a vital part of my academic plan, which helped me get through both my undergraduate and graduate studies. Since graduation, while working as an academic support specialist in higher education, I have learned additional strategies or actions that could positively or negatively impact a student's efforts. These new strategies, which mostly arose from technology changes, include the following:

- **If you email a paper to a professor check to see if the email was success-**

fully sent. Look in your 'Sent' folder and verify the correct paper was attached. You should also consider asking the professor to email you to verify the paper was received. Another option is to copy the message to your own email address. You'd be amazed at the amount of students who thought they clicked 'Send' only to find the paper never left their 'Draft' folder.

- **Use an appropriate email address when sending messages out to professors.** First of all, email usernames that are vulgar or in anyway "inappropriate" may be seen as possible spam, which a professor will likely delete without opening if her/his Spam filter doesn't delete the email first. Additionally, creating inappropriate usernames may make a professor question your dedication to the class; never a good thing to do. Be safe and just use your campus email.

- **If you have a cell phone, reconsider whether or not you need a landline as well.** Remember, money doesn't grow on trees. If you have a cell, what difference will the landline truly make; save your money.

- **Keep magnets away from computers, credit cards, memory cards, flash drives and other technological devices.** Even the smallest magnets can erase hard drives through minimal contact, wiping out any saved papers. Best to leave magnets for holding papers and notes to fridges.

- **Close out of all screens and "logout" when using public computers.** Failing to completely logout could leave your personal information vulnerable to identity theft not to mention someone could access your saved papers.

- **Don't say your passwords or private identification numbers out loud, especially when in line at Student Accounts or at the Financial Aid Office.** Identity theft happens more than you'd think. A student standing nearby could overhear your password or other private information if you say it out loud. Instead, write the information on a slip of paper and hand that over to the staff member requesting it. Afterwards, get the slip of paper back and shred it. Do not keep a list of passwords, your Social Security Card or your personal identification numbers on you. That way, if you lose your wallet or whatever you kept that private information in, no one will have access to this sensitive data.

- **Scan any flash drive, email attachment or questionable file for viruses BEFORE opening on your computer.** Doing so will lessen the chance of a virus erasing your computer's files.

- **Make a backup of research papers and other important documents periodically.** When working on my Master's thesis, my computer crashed. Since I had no backup, I lost the chapters I had completed and polished. If I had simply made a back up on a separate drive, I would have easily recovered what was lost, or at least most of it. My advice, get a flash drive with a minimum of 10 gigabytes to use for periodically backing up files. Then, have a second flash drive that you use for day to day writing/modifying of papers.

- **Make sure you empty your pockets before doing laundry.** While money usually survives a trip through the washing machine, flash drives, cell phones and small notebooks usually don't do so well.

Final Thoughts

After I provide this advice to students, I often hear statements like "why didn't anyone ever tell me about these study techniques before?" In some cases, students were provided study advice, but it was during college orientation the week before the student's first semester begins. As that is an exciting and extremely stressful time, it's no wonder study skills get lost in the shuffle to get through the first couple weeks. It is my sincere hope that students reading this book will give these strategies a try. From decades of experience as a tutor and a professor, I have found that students employing these strategies do significantly better in their class assessments and retain course material for use later in their professional career. That said, there is one last suggestion I'd like to make. No matter how stressful college gets, never give up and never stop striving for the A's. With dedication, focus and a willingness to ask for help, any college student can succeed.

www.ingramcontent.com/pod-product-compliance
Lightning Source LLC
Chambersburg PA
CBHW070456100426
42743CB00010B/1638